D1621130

this book
belongs to FLIP .

11-14

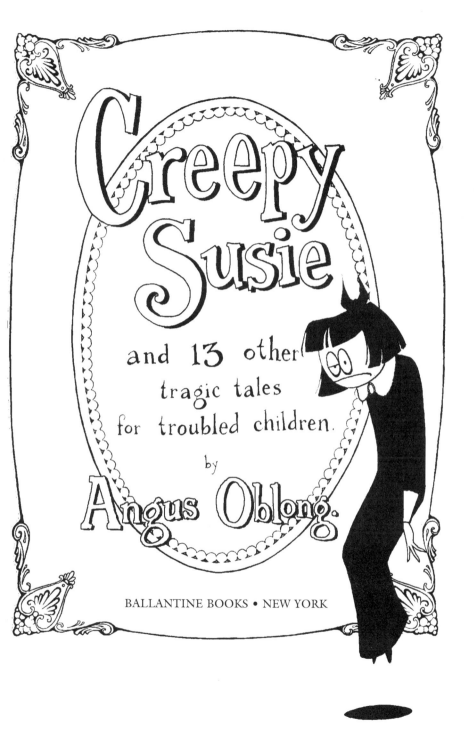

Creepy Susie

and 13 other tragic tales for troubled children.

by

Angus Oblong

BALLANTINE BOOKS • NEW YORK

A Ballantine Book
Published by The Ballantine Publishing Group

www.randomhouse.com/BB/

Library of Congress Cataloging-in-Publication Data

Oblong, Angus
    Creepy Susie : and 13 other tragic tales for troubled children / Angus Oblong
        p. cm.
    ISBN 0-345-43301-7 (alk. paper)
    1. Children Humor. 2. Problem children Humor. I. Title
    PN6231.C32024   1999
    741.5'973—dc21   99-23482
                                     CIP

Manufactured in the United States of America

First Edition: October 1999

10 9 8 7 6 5 4 3 2 1

this book is
dedicated to
Tiffany, Kirsten,
Riley, Clayton & Gage,
my nieces & nephews.

CONTENTS

Creepy Susie

and 13 other
tragic tales
for troubled children.

This is Helga.

These are the Debbies.
The Debbies all tried very hard
to be the same.

Helga was an endless source of amusement to the Debbies...

tee hee
hee hee
hee

Even though Helga was different, she had somehow convinced herself that there was a place in society for her.

The Debbies sought to destroy Helga's glimmer of hope to one day fit in.

Helga became obsessed with the thought of revenge.

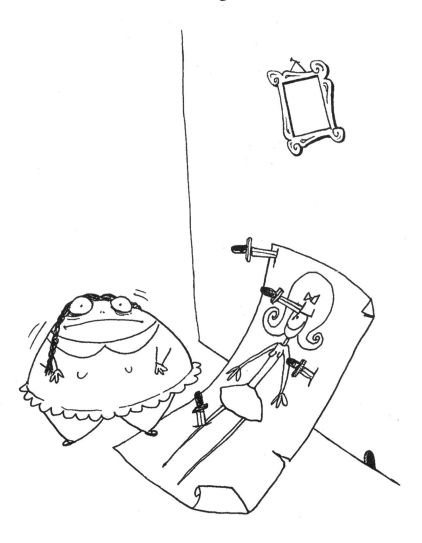

Helga disguised herself as a Debbie
& mingled among them.

Once inside the clique,
  Helga began studying their
itty bitty thoughts &
their migration patterns.

Over lunch,
the Debbies decided to
have a slumber party
at Debbie's house.

They ate pizza, painted their toenails pink, giggled & talked about Matthew Kelly's excellent butt cheeks.

While the Debbies slept Helga snipped off their annoying little heads.

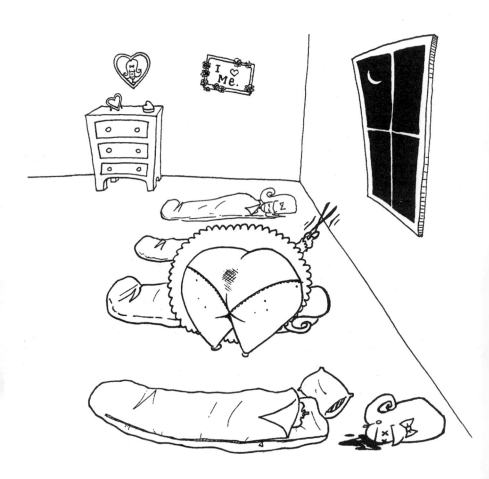

Then she ate all of the
pizza crusts.

— the end.

16

18

28

Morning came &
Betsy turned to ashes.

there once was a boy
from Nantucket,

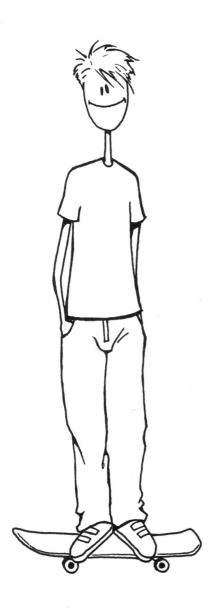

His name
was Waldo.

Waldo's best friend was his dog, Bean.   Bean had no legs & no tail. He looked just like a big bean with a dog head.

While out on a walk one day, Bean made a poo that looked just like himself.

"We'll be famous!"
   squealed Waldo.

Waldo rushed the poo home
to show his mother.

She was drunk.

She hit Waldo
with a big
frozen meat.

She shoved Bean
into a drawer,

She
destroyed
the
poo…

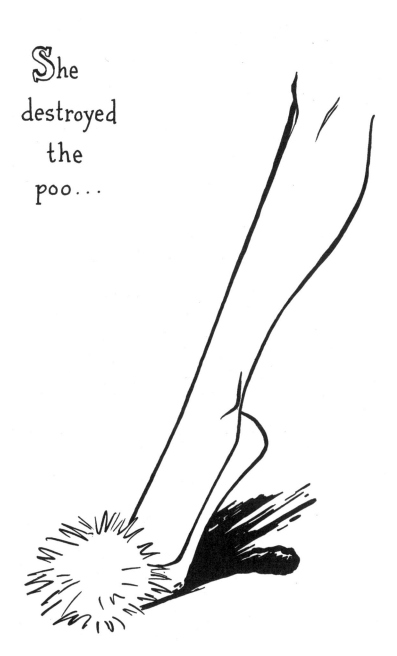

hen she threw up.

the end...

Little Scooter

 HERE WAS JUST SOMETHING ABOUT SCOOTER...

...THAT MADE PEOPLE WANT TO
THROW THINGS AT HIS HEAD.

ANYTHING THEY COULD GET THEIR HANDS ON.

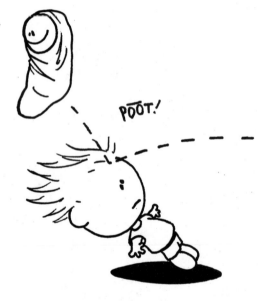

POOT!

 LL DAY.

E VERY DAY.

Even mrs. bump...

BIFF

AFTER YEARS OF THIS, SCOOTER WAS DIAGNOSED WITH A LOOSE BRAIN.

rattle
rattle
rattle
rattle

THE DOCTOR THOUGHT IT BEST
THAT SCOOTER BE PUT TO SLEEP.

— THE END.

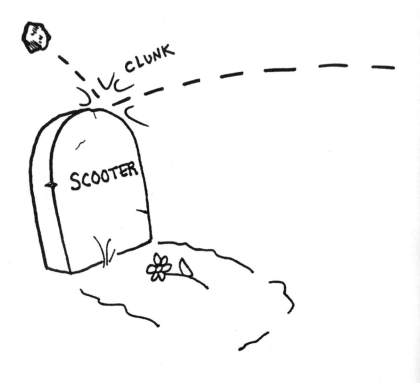

Little Sammy was a <u>happy</u> <u>happy</u> boy!!

...too damn happy...

Everything Sammy saw made him happier. everything. (⟹.)

gum on the sidewalk...

gigantic butts...

homosexuals...

...mutant babies,

... bunnies & flowers
& all that is
politically correct.

It was simple, really.

Sammy had to be *stopped!*

$\mathcal{S}$ammy was cured with
electroshock therapy.

And thank God he grew up to be normal.

— the end.

Milo's disorder.

Milo wasn't like other boys...

Milo thought that maybe
there was a monster
in the toilet watching his butt.

He was certain that when he
   turned away,
the things behind him smiled.

He knew all about the ~~diner waitress~~ serpent that lived under his bed.

And while he slept
his head would bloom open to let the fish out.

Milo was cured with
electroshock therapy.

And thank God he grew up to be normal.

the end!

There was something a little creepy about Susie...

...**P**ERHAPS it was HER collection of dead rats & chickens.

Or maybe it was that she never smiled,

Unless she was holding something slimy.

the rest of Susie's family
was perfectly normal.

Except for HER father, WHO WAS A midget albino cross dresser...

It came to pass that one day
Eric Twinklebutt developed a
schoolboy crush on Susie.

She Did Not know
wHat To do...

So sHe igNOREd hiM...

Susie's vagina tingled at the
thought of Eric Twinklebutt
but she still did not know
what to do.

She read one of those
Romance Novels but
she threw up.

....Susie went to see
Her great-great-great-
grandmother Ruby.

... to ask for Advice ON boys.

·But Great-great-great-grandmother Ruby was no help at all because she'd been dead for a long long time...

So susie decided to take care of the problem.

— the end.

Emily,
amputee.

Emily went to her doctor for her annual checkup.

Some paperwork got mixed up & they amputated one of her legs...

- the end.

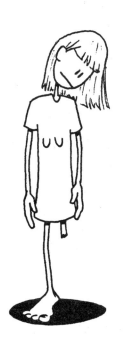

Narcoleptic Scottie.

Little Scottie was born a dog.

He was short...

very very short.

Scottie often dreamt
he was tall.

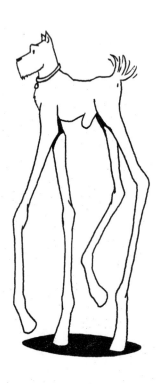

He sometimes dreamt he was human.

Scottie hated
being a dog...

Begging for food was
downright undignified ...

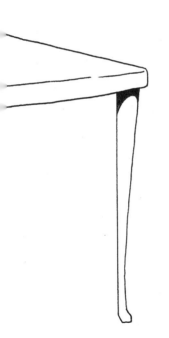

... and hardly worth it.

$\mathcal{S}$cottie enjoyed
sleeping & dreaming.

He dreamt &
dreamt &
dreamt.

Z..

He became narcoleptic.

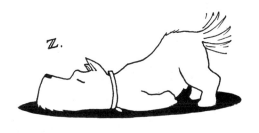

The family thought that
Scottie was dead...

And they buried
him in
the backyard.

– the end.

Sibling Rivalry...

Tommy & Patty were brother
& sister. They hated each other.

Tommy put a poo & booger
sandwich in Patty's lunch pail.

So Patty put glue
on the toilet seat.

So Tommy told all of
Patty's friends that she
was a hermaphrodite.

So Patty told Tommy that mommy & daddy were killed in a horrible accident.

So Tommy baked Mittens
at 350°, to a light golden brown.

So Patty put a rake
through Tommy's skull
while he was watching Saturday
morning cartoons.

And Patty was an only child.

-the end.

Rosie's Crazy Mother.

Rosie's mother was a crazy woman.

She shaved the cats,

... then she glued little
pictures of Elvis all
over them.

Rosie's crazy mother had a
life-sized tattoo of herself
on her back "just in case."

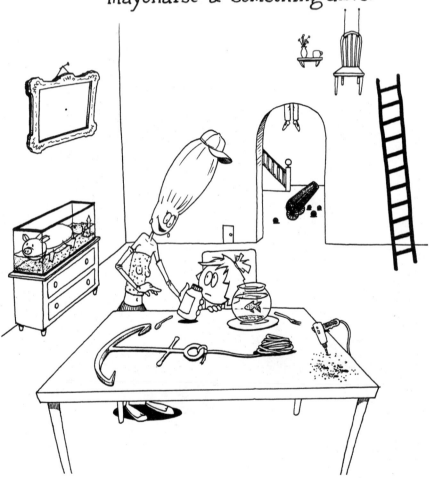

After-school snacks usually consisted of a jar of mayonaise & something alive.

Rosie finally decided
that it was weird that
her mother made her
sleep in the oven.

She feared she would
grow up to be
just like her mother.

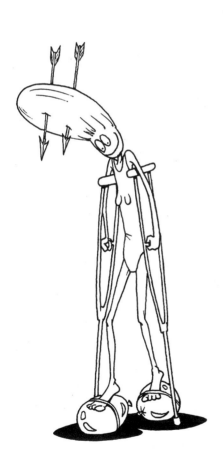

JENNY,
JENNY,
JENNY
& BABETTE,
the siamese quadruplets.

$\mathcal{J}$enny, Jenny, Jenny & Babette
weren't like the other
children …

the neighborhood children
wouldn't play with them
because they looked too odd.

Even the deformed children stared in disbelief.

Their father feared them...

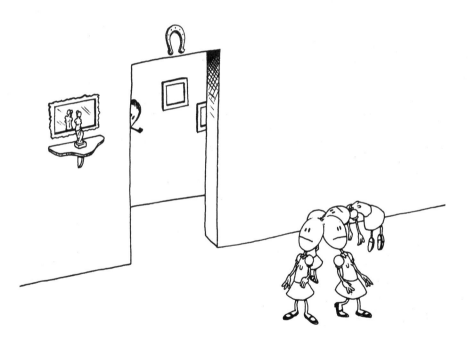

Their mother thought they were a great big spider.

Jenny, Jenny, Jenny & Babette ran away from home to start a new life.

A normal life.

They got a job,

They got a car,

they got married
to a pervert,

they had their 7th birthday.
They'd never been happier.

Jenny, Jenny, Jenny & Babette
put on a disguise & went
back to their old neighborhood.

Oh how they loathed
their parents...

So they cooked &
ate them.

— the end.

dick & muffy.

145

151

Mary had a little Chainsaw.

Mary had a little chainsaw...

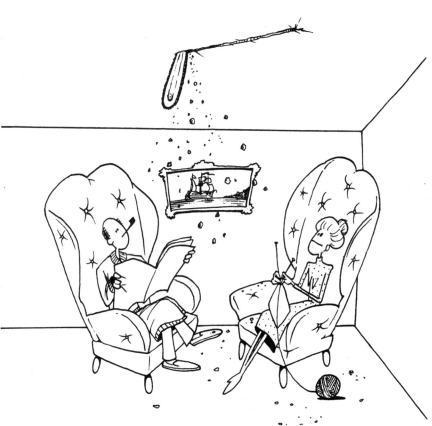

Its teeth were sharp
as steel.

Everywhere that Mary went,
the saw was sure to go.

palindrome.

$\mathcal{S}$he brought it with her
to school one day.

Which apparently was against the rules...

$\mathbf{I}$t made the children laugh & play
to see a chainsaw at school.

Mary grew up to be one of those
big biker women with tattoos.

— the end.

Angus Oblong is a writer & illustrator residing in San Francisco, CA, and does not live in L.A. Besides this series of dark & twisted tales in the guise of children's books, he also writes & illustrates children's books meant for children.

Angus Oblong is legally insane & an avid collector of dead trees which clutter his tiny non-lit studio apartment. His fascination with physical deformities stems from the fact that a living, movable right hand is growing from the center of his back. Otherwise, he is perfectly normal.